Psalm 73–Sight

PERSPECTIVE ALTERING

Yolanda "Cookie" Doyle

ISBN 979-8-88540-584-3 (paperback)
ISBN 979-8-88540-585-0 (digital)

Christian Faith Publishing
832 Park Avenue
Meadville, PA 16335
www.christianfaithpublishing.com

CONTENTS

SIGHT: PERSPECTIVE ALTERING

This study will take us through various texts of Scripture that allow us to look into the lives of many who struggled with a direction God allowed in their lives. We will look at men such as Habakkuk, Asaph, and David. We will see how these men handled circumstances outside their control. How does what they see alter their perspective? God tells us to walk by faith and not by sight for a reason. The fact that our senses can lead us down a wrong path that questions God's goodness is seen throughout Scripture.

We will take a glimpse at postexilic Israel and how they were facing the consequences of their sin. Their struggles were due to their rebellion. What they saw was meant to call them to repentance. Instead, it caused them to be sorry they ever followed God. God would not relent. He waited for them to, but they only lifted their fists to him. You probably know someone like that. Someone who faced the consequences for their sin, but instead of repenting, they hardened. It does not have to end this way. God knows sight can cause us to slip. That is why we are directed to walk by faith. Our sight almost always alters our perspective.

Separating everyday life in a sinful world and the things we see that can cause us to almost slip must be distinguished from God's hand of discipline for rebellion. Both can look the same, but if we stay sensitive to God's Spirit, we can know that what we see is never meant to cause us to slip. Each circumstance calls us to different things: *(1)* to walk by faith or *(2)* repentance. Neither situation ever calls us to count on what we see. Sight is perspective altering. It is not dependable. We will see that in this study. Let's let God teach us how to trust what he says and not what we see. He wants to. Will you let him?

We must begin with the fact that God is good. His desire is for us, not for our harm. He wants our repentance, righteousness, and a life that forms us into the image of his Son (*Romans 8:28–30*).

Thank you for choosing this journey. Let's begin with God. After all, everything should begin there.

PSALM OF ASAPH

Psalm 73 (NKJV)

Truly God *is* good to Israel,
To such as are pure in heart.
But as for me, my feet had almost stumbled;
My steps had nearly slipped.
For I *was* envious of the boastful,
When I saw the prosperity of the wicked.
For *there are* no pangs in their death,
But their strength *is* firm.
They *are* not in trouble *as other* men,
Nor are they plagued like *other* men.
Therefore pride serves as their necklace;
Violence covers them *like* a garment.
Their eyes bulge with abundance;
They have more than heart could wish.
They scoff and speak wickedly *concerning* oppression;
They speak loftily.
They set their mouth against the heavens,
And their tongue walks through the earth.

Therefore his people return here,
And waters of a full *cup* are drained by them.
And they say, "How does God know?
And is there knowledge in the most High?"
Behold, these *are* the ungodly,
Who are always at ease;
They increase *in* riches.
surely I have cleansed my heart *in* vain,
And washed my hands in innocence.
For all day long I have been plagued,
And chastened every morning.

If I had said, "I will speak thus,"
Behold, I would have been untrue to the generation of Your children.
When I thought *how* to understand this,
It *was* too painful for me—
Until I went into the sanctuary of God;
Then I understood their end.
Surely You set them in slippery places;
You cast them down to destruction.
Oh, how they are *brought* to desolation, as in a moment!
They are utterly consumed with terrors.
As a dream when *one* awakes,
So, Lord, when You awake,
You shall despise their image.
Thus my heart was grieved,
And I was vexed in my mind.
I *was* so foolish and ignorant;

I was *like* a beast before You.
Nevertheless I *am* continually with You;
You hold *me* by my right hand.
You will guide me with Your counsel,
And afterward receive me *to* glory.
Whom have I in heaven *but You?*
And *there is* none upon earth *that* I desire besides You.
My flesh and my heart fail;
But God *is* the strength of my heart and my portion forever.
For indeed, those who are far from You shall perish;
You have destroyed all those who desert You for harlotry.
But *it is* good for me to draw near to God;
I have put my trust in the Lord God,
That I may declare all Your works.

LESSON ONE

God Is Good, Isn't He?

I.

Read *Psalm 73*. On a separate sheet, outline this Psalm. Do a little research on it.

This Psalm is attributed to Asaph. Who was Asaph? Read the following passages and write down what you learn.

1 Chronicles 6:29–32, 39 ___________________________________

____

1 Chronicles 16:4–5 _______________________________________

2 Chronicles 5:11–14 _______________________________________

____

What particular ministries could you substitute Asaph's ministry with today? ____

____

If you knew someone in this position who struggled in their faith, even just for a moment in time, would you think it easier to share when you may be struggling with your faith? _______________

____

Someone you respect sharing that they are wrestling with God and their faith may help you not feel alone. Too often, leaders come across so strong. It is possible they seem unrelatable in areas of struggle. *Read 1 Corinthians 10:13.* How does this help you? _____________

____

____

II.
Write out *Psalm 73:1.* ________________________________

____

Write what you think "God is good" means? ________________

____

Let's look at a few passages and how they define God's goodness. Write out or paraphrase each verse.
Psalm 34:8 ______________________________________
Psalm 145:9 _____________________________________
James 1:17 ______________________________________

Let's look at God's goodness in creation. Seven times God's goodness is expressed as he speaks the creation into existence. *Read Genesis 1:4, 10, 12, 18, 21, 25, 31.* How do these passages help you understand God's goodness? ______________________________

____

____

III.
To say that God is good is to declare that he always acts in right, true, and good ways. Goodness is a fruit of the Spirit. Goodness is

displayed as a part of his character. This is an attribute he shares with those who become his children. God's nature is good. He cannot contradict his nature.

List a few things you have been through that may have caused you, even slightly, to question God's goodness.

1. ____

2. ____

3. ____

How did you come in contact with God's goodness in those difficulties? If not, have you since looked back and now see it? __________

____

God's *common grace* or his *general goodness* is expressed in Scripture. *Read Matthew 5:43–45* and paraphrase it. __________________

____

How does this open up your understanding of God's goodness? ____

____

____

IV.

Look back at Psalm 73:1; what do you think Asaph means, *"to those who are pure in heart?"*

____

Read Matthew 5:8. What does this verse say about the "pure in heart?"

____

____

Read Hebrews 12:14. Who will see God in this passage? _____________

What is the connection between these verses? _______________________
____

How do you think the more pinpointed experience of the goodness of God in Psalm 73:1 *differs* from what we studied on God's common goodness? ____
____
____

From all you looked at this week, what have you learned? What has challenged or encouraged you?_________________________________

What are some *myths* that are connected to God's goodness in your thinking? ____
____

What are some things you've *experienced* that stand in the way of understanding that God is truly good? ________________________
____
____
What do the answers of the last two questions reveal about you? ___
____

V.

Day of prayer

As we look more thoroughly at Asaph's Psalm, we will see he is more like you and me than we could imagine.

End your time with prayer. Be honest about your perspective. Maybe by faith you can say, "Lord, I am doing this study so something in me wants to put my entire weight into the reality that you are good. I will remain teachable." Or "Lord, I know you are good. I know there is something you want to teach me. I am listening."

Thank you for your perseverance! Let's meet again next week.

LESSON TWO

Do Not Walk by Sight

I.

Read *Psalm 73.*

Write out the *first 4 words* of Psalm 73:1, then verse 2.______________

____

It is possible that you are living the psalmist reality. Perhaps you have the knowledge that God is good. Unfortunately, many of us don't stop there. Asaph says, *"But as for me, my feet had almost slipped."* He used the conjunction *but. But* is used to connect ideas that *contrast.*

Let's look at a familiar biblical personality where we see this contrast. Read *Jonah 1:1–6.* Explain the *but* (the contrast) between God and Jonah. Why should this matter?______________________

____

When we are contrasted with God in Scripture, it is always that we are less, wrong, or in doubt. Remember, anything good about us is from God. Read *Galatians 5:22–23.* What is the good that comes from God? ______________________________________

____

Let's look at Asaph's contrast of himself to God's goodness. Read *Psalm 73:3–12*. Write out some of Asaph's complaints. ____________

____

How do things that seem out of line with God's goodness alter your perspective? ____

____

II.

Write out *Psalm 73:3* ______________________________________

____

How does envy reveal itself through you? _______________________

____

Look up the Hebrew word for *envy* and share that definition. ______

____

Envy is a feeling of discontent or resentment based on what someone else has. It is a strong desire to have the same things someone else has.

What was the consequences for Asaph's envy? ___________________

____

Our frustrations with God or the world around us have consequences when not handled biblically. Let's look at a few passages where the expression of frustration is loud and clear. *Romans 15:4, "For whatever was written in former days was written for our instruction, that through endurance and through the encouragement of the Scriptures we might have hope."*

Read Habakkuk 1:1–4. What was Habakkuk's complaint? _________
____
What are the similarities in how Habakkuk and Asaph expressed envy? ____
____

Envy is in line with coveting, which is the tenth commandment. Unlike the other commandments, which focus on outward actions, this commandment focuses on the condition of the heart. The other nine commandments focus on doing a forbidden action, while this one focuses on inward thoughts.
What do you think are the similarities or differences between envy and coveting? ____
____

What area(s) in your life is God revealing a problem with envy? ____
____

We should never make something acceptable that God hates. God gives examples in his Word for our encouragement. We can walk through these lessons and see how others failed or were victorious and learn. The purpose of Scripture is that we may learn who God is; that is foremost. Then we learn what humanity is in relationship to God. God reveals areas where repentance is needed. *Is envy an area you need to confess and repent?* _________________________________

We cannot avoid situations that bring the emotion of envy, but we will learn how to deal with them biblically. Having the emotion is not a sin. *Nursing the emotion is.*

III.
Read Psalm *73:2–13,* write out verse *13.* _______________________

____

Wow! That is a strong declaration! Have you ever felt like your walk with the Lord was futile? What were you dealing with? ___________

____

What changed? How have you adjusted your thinking to line up with Scripture? ____

____

It is easy to feel condemned if you ever felt in any real way that your service for the Lord is futile. Write out a prayer of confession. ______

____

When doubt takes hold of us in a way that makes us point the finger at God and accuse him of not being good, we sin. We call him a liar. When we see any circumstance as not going our way and then feel like God owes us or isn't dealing with us fairly, we make ourselves a god.

That is sin and must be confessed. Read *Psalm 96:4–5.* What does verse 4 call all other gods? _________________________________

God stands ready to embrace us and to give us confidence that he knows what he is doing. Our circumstances may be his work to turn us from sin or he's redirecting us for ministry. We must keep our eyes on God, not our circumstances. Sight will alter our perspective.

IV.

One more example that will help us understand tough situations can bring thoughts that don't line up with God's character like we saw with Habakkuk and Asaph.

Read *Job 2:1–8, 3:1–12.* Who initiates the hardship in Job's life? ___ What does he express in his frustration? _______________________________

____

Can you relate to Job? ____
Is there something you are going through or have gone through that has caused you to express the depth of emotion that Job was expressing? *Briefly share.* ____

____

How have you been able to see the goodness of God in the circumstance or since? ____

____

End this lesson by rehearsing the reality that God is good. Rehearsing just means finding passages that declare that truth and then writing them and keeping it before you in a tangible way.
List a passage(s) that you find about God's goodness. Write them out here or on an index card. Meditate on those verses the rest of the week. ____

____

V.

Asaph's attention shifted from God to the wicked. His entire perspective changed. Life no longer looked the same. There were some obvious inequities he did not understand. The more he looked at the wicked, the more troubled he became. His theology didn't seem to make much sense anymore. He began to wonder and waver. In taking his eyes off God's goodness, his testimony goes to doubt and uncertainty.

We observe the world today and the cacophony of negative that comes from almost every direction. What are the hidden thoughts of your heart? ____

____

The way you share can affect your testimony. *Read Luke 6:45.* What accountability does this verse offer? ______________________
What are your words saying about your view of God? __________

____

Have you ever struggled with a problem and decided to keep it between you and God for the sake of others? Explain. __________

____

Let's end this week by thanking God for all you have observed and learned. In just a sentence or two, what are you grateful for? ______

____

It's been a great week. Keep persevering!

LESSON THREE

Trials, Trials, Trials

I.

Everyone who is part of the kingdom of God will face trials. Inequity is a part of our sinful world. It is used as a trial, even the discipline of God's children. The next two weeks, we will look at how God uses trials for his children.

Read *Psalm 73:1–12*. Briefly write out what Asaph's trial was. _______

____

Do his circumstances seem self-inflicted? Explain your answer. _____

____

Remember, no matter how you answered that question, Asaph's circumstances still impacted him to the point of envy and almost slipping. There are more reasons for trials than we will cover. I just want us to look at some that may be more valuable for us.

Trials produce perseverance and hope. Read the following passage and write out or paraphrase.

James 1:2–4, 12 _______________________________

____

Read a few commentaries to understand what it means to *"remain steadfast."* Write out what you find. _______________________

____

Think of the trial you are facing now. What would look different if you *"remained steadfast under* (your) *trial?"* _______________

____

*Romans 8:18–30*_______________________________

____

Knowing that God's purpose for our trials is to *conform us into the image of his Son (v. 29),* where is his image most visible as you deal with your trial? *Galatians 5:22–23* may help you answer. _________

____

II.
Trials remind us that our boast should be only *in the Lord.* Read the following passage and write out or paraphrase the text.

1 Corinthians 1:28–31 _________________________

____

Prayer is vital when we are going through a trial. Over the years, I have found that many people are quick to ask for prayer, but only few share the answers to those prayers. Sadly, many forget God even answered. When God answers our prayers, we must stop and recognize how he got us through.

Write down some sentiments folks expressed that focus more on the one sharing a struggle than on God, i.e., *"You've got this!"* _________

____

How easy is it to allow those sentiments to take your attention off "boasting in the Lord" and putting success on yourself? _________

____

III.
Trials are used to discipline God's children. Read the following passages and write out or paraphrase.

Hebrews 12:5–10 _______________________________

____

Reread the last part of verse 10. What is his discipline for? _________

____

Psalm 139:23–24, 19:13–14 _____________________

____

These psalms are reflective of a child toward a loving parent. Another great analogy could be anything that expresses a person who is desperately surrendered to their Lord.

What needs to change for these psalms to reflect your heart? We need to live with an expectation of the loving discipline of our Father. He must bring his holiness out of each of his children. _____________

IV.

Trials come simply because we live in a broken world. This is pretty much where Asaph landed. Life happens! God's Word offers us a scriptural landing strip. Read the following passages and write out or paraphrase.

1 Peter 3:14–15 ______________________________

____

Psalm 27:14 ______________________________

____

1 John 4:4 ______________________________

____

Don't believe the lie that God's children should have health and wealth. It is a lie that has caused discouragement and depression in many of God's children. This is the direction Asaph was headed. The great thing about Psalm 73 and why I picked it to study is it's a blueprint on how to get through trials successfully. Yet it offers us an example of a real walk through a trial. It offers directions we can follow.

V.

Read Psalm 73.

Next week, we will look at trials that happen when we sin. Trials that fall under the "discipline" of God. We will examine what happens to us if we refuse to pay attention to what God is trying to correct.

Write out *Psalm 73:2.* ______________________________

____

Think through such an honest confession. What's the difference, if any, between Asaph stating this reality verses grumbling? _________

____

Asaph *"almost slipped."* This is serious. Unfortunately, many actually do. What trials may have caused you to *"almost slip?"* _________

____

Replace Asaph's word *slipped* with how you felt at the time you struggled, *"I almost* _______________________________

____*"*

What put you back on track? ____________________

Next week, we will look at those who do slip, sadly.

Thanks for a job well done! Keep persevering!

LESSON FOUR

Senses, the Caboose

I.

Read Psalm 73. Write out *verse 3.* _______________________

____

Here's the transition in Asaph's testimony:

Truly God is good
But as for me
For I was envious
When I saw the...

We have already looked at the fact that Asaph understood that God was good. The *but* contrasted Asaph from God. Asaph took his eyes off what he knew would keep him steady. He allowed what he saw to almost cause him to slip.

Why was the sense of sight huge in altering Asaph's perspective? ____

____

Let's land here for a short investigation of what God's Word says about the ease of slipping when we take our eyes off him.

Read Genesis 3:1–7. What is the progression in *verse 6* that brought about Eve's sinful actions? _______________________________

James 1:14–15. How do our worldly desires cause us to sin? ________

____

Where does the responsibility lie when we choose to follow our senses to sinful actions? _______________________________________

____

Read Mark 9:43–47. While we need to know that Jesus was speaking metaphorically here, what is he teaching? Read a commentary or two to help. ____

____

As a mom of five, a grandmother of six, and a preschool teacher, I taught the lesson of emotions/senses being our caboose thousands of times. I will not use my preschool teacher's voice to remind us of the dangers of being led by our emotions/senses. Think of it like this, Eve had the whole human race in the hands of her senses. She ate the fruit, and her children suffer because of what she chose to see, touch, and taste.

Every man and woman who ever walked the Earth suffers at her expense. I know Scripture speaks of Adam's failure, but we must remember Eve was the catalyst. And yes, every one of us would have been led by our senses and abdicated walking with God in the Garden of Eden too. No need to have that conversation.

II.

We will briefly look at the ultimate success story. *Read Matthew 4:1–11*. I am sure after reading this you may be thinking, *Well, duh, it's Jesus.* But we cannot forget we are looking at Jesus in his humanity. We must read this with the lesson in mind it is meant to teach. Jesus, filled with the Spirit, did not capitulate to his senses. God's children filled with his Spirit can be successful too.

Who led him to his test? ___________________________________

What made his flesh vulnerable? _____________________________

How did Jesus bring his flesh into submission? _________________

How persistent was the enemy (number of temptations)? _________

How was Jesus encouraged when it was over? __________________

How was God's presence involved throughout the testing? _______

____

Read Psalm 34:4, 6, 7, 15–19. What does God do for those who look to him? ____

____

Share a time you went with sight and sinned? How did your story end? ____

____

III.

In this next session, we will look at the disaster of allowing our senses to lead. We already saw a little with Eve. There were great consequences. I want to dig into Malachi. Before we go there, remember we have Jesus's success in Matthew 4 and know that was recorded for our hope. It is a story that can be ours. We will see that Asaph's is a story of success too. However, it is vital that we understand the hardening that can happen if we don't take this subject seriously.

Read the *book of Malachi*. Look up a summary of this book. In a few sentences, write out what you learn. _______________________

____

Here's what I have in a few sentences. After losing their homeland to invaders due to their sin, the Jews are back home, rebuilding their nation, and back to sinning their way into God's discipline. Life is complicated, and their enemies are more successful than they are. Instead of looking at themselves and seeing the trials coming from a God who wants to bring them to repentance, they accuse God of evil motives.

Bookmark Malachi. Read Psalm 73:1–12 to remind ourselves what Asaph saw and struggled with. Take time to pray and journal what God speaks to your heart.

From Malachi, finish the passages *(NKJV):*

1:2 "I have loved you," says the Lord, "Yet you say, "_______________

___________________________________?""

1:6d Says the Lord of host, "To you priests who despise My name. Yet you say, "______________________________

___________________________________?""

1:7a "You offer defiled food on My altar, but say, "_______________

___________________________________?""

Paraphrase *7b–8.* _____________________________________

____

They are arguing with God. They are in disobedience; what are they doing wrong? For more insight, read *Deuteronomy 15:21, 17:1; Leviticus 22:21–25.*_______________________________

____

IV.

The Nation of Israel is facing hard times because God is not willing to accept their sin. He isn't allowing his children to prosper, but their enemies are prospering. Instead of turning from their sin, they are hardened by what they *see* and *experience*. God was using their trials to turn their eyes and hearts back to him. He wanted them to remember his promises; in juxtaposition, they hardened and sinned all the more. *Read Malachi 3:13–15. Paraphrase verses 13–14.*_______

____

Write out verse 15. _______________________________

____

How similar is their complaint to Asaph's? _______________

____

Let's look back at the warning. Instead of humbling themselves, they blamed God. *They refused to see the goodness of God.* Yesterday, we studied some reasons for trials. That was so we are not discouraged, and like Israel in Malachi, forget *God is GOOD.* I desire to help us avoid the kind of frustration that leads to anger, then ends in hardened hearts. In *verse 14,* they said, *"It is useless to serve God; what profit is it that we have kept His ordinance?"*

What brings a person who belongs to the Lord to a place of this kind of accusation? ____

____

V.

Let's end our week by looking at an example in the New Testament. Walking with Jesus is one thing; continuing to abide may be thwarted by a few different things, persecution because of commitment to him, worldliness, and shallow roots. As we saw in Malachi, Israel rejected God because they wanted him to change before they would. His requirement was for their repentance before he'd relent. God asks us to walk by faith, even when sight is confusing. Sometimes sight can come from what we hear, then picture it as confusing, and we imagine it being too complicated. Let's see how Scripture explains this.

Read John 6:25–70. Summarize this story from *verses 47–59.* ______

____

What specifically was Jesus's teaching concerning *"the bread and the wine?"* ____

____

From the NIV translation, complete this statement, *v. 60. "This is a hard teaching* ____

____ *?"*

There are differences between saying, *"Who can understand it?"* versus *"Who can accept it?"*

What do you think those differences are? _________________________
_______________________________________ Why does it matter?
____

Many of his disciples chose not to accept this teaching; what did they do, *verse 66?* ____
____

In *verse 67,* you can see that Jesus understood this was a difficult teaching. What did he ask of the twelve? _______________________

In *verse 68,* when Peter responds, does he address the teaching that Jesus just gave? ____

How did Peter answer? _______________________________________
____

What does Peter's answer say about his sight? _________________
____

Peter chose to trust in who he believed Jesus was and let go of what he could not understand. His faith became sight, and he gained an understanding of what Jesus was telling them about eating his body and drinking his blood. *Read Matthew 26:26–29.* Here, Peter's faith came full circle. That does not always happen here on earth. Asaph had to go back to *"God is good"* and leave it at that. David went back to *"wait on the Lord,"* knowing there is stability in the Lord. Write any final thoughts that come to you after doing this lesson. _______
____

<h1 style="text-align:center">LESSON FIVE</h1>

There Is, Therefore, No Condemnation

I.

Last week, we were left contemplating the hardening that can happen when led by the things we see or experience that seem contrary to the goodness of God toward those "pure in heart." This week, I'd like to continue to probe Israel from Malachi, Habakkuk, and Asaph's views of the world around them. The vast amount of our study will remind us of God's good *desire* toward us, even if we persist in the stubbornness of our senses. We can thwart him from giving us his good desires if we persist, but that isn't what he wants.

Read Psalm 73:1–14. Paraphrase your answers.

What did Asaph see, *verses 3–12?* _______________________

____

How did he express his discouragement, *verses 13–14?* _________

____

Read Habakkuk 1:1–4.

What was Habakkuk experiencing? _______________________

____

What do you think was the tone of his questions? _________________

Read Malachi 2:17.

God was wearied by the people's accusations. From this verse, what were those accusations? ____

Is there an experience in your past or present that relates to the remarks made in these passages? _______________________________

____

How might your experience distort your view of God? ___________

____

How did it grow your confidence in God's goodness? ____________

____

II.

Sadly, what we looked at in part *I* tends to be the view of more Christians than not. While Scripture encourages and commands God's children to *"walk by faith and not by sight,"* sight may be the primary contingent that sabotages us from day to day. We find that our faith vacillates, and we *almost slip* more frequently than we'd like.

The heart of God is not that we slip nor is it our condemnation but the sanctification of his children. Let's see what Scripture says.

Read and paraphrase the following passages.

1 Thessalonians 4:3a _______________________________________

Psalm 16:11 ____

____

Jeremiah 3:22 ____

____

1 John 1:9 _______________________________________

____

These passages express God's heart yet while communicating a responsibility on our part. Write in your own words the responsibility we have in order to experience the fullness of God's joy. ________

____

III.

Let's look at how the heart of our good God is expressed to Israel in Malachi, even while the people are arguing that God is not good. The verses you are about to read have to do with tithing. This lesson is not going into the debate on tithing under the new covenant. The purpose of what you will see is that while the people are still wearying God with their accusations, he expresses his desire to bless them if they would only turn from their sin and do righteously. *Read Malachi 3:8–12.* What is God's desire for his children? _________________

____

Was there a requirement for them to receive God's pinpointed goodness? ____

____

While many continued to complain harshly against God, many chose to refocus their senses, repent, and obediently submit. *Read Malachi 3:16–18.* We will see how quickly God moves on their behalf. He doesn't condemn them. How do we know this is true?
Read verse 17 and paraphrase. __________________________

____

How does this help you understand the heart of God? ________

____

IV.

Read Psalm 73. I hope the detours of the last few weeks from Psalm 73 have been roads worth traveling for you. We are back to examine how Asaph handled his point of view. By way of reminder, *read verses 1–3. List Asaph's declarations.*

____

____

____

Read verse 15. The psalmist considered speaking openly about his doubts and dilemma. He chose not to. Why? __________________

____

Verse 15 allows us to conclude that the points of view, *verses 4–12,* were pondered and weighed in Asaph's heart. It is much easier to share our sinful points of view and possible accusations against God openly. We are asked to carry one another's burdens. Those burdens are a separate issue from accusations we might make against God due to what we see going on in the world around us. Now those points of view may need to be shared with a biblical counselor. We *cannot* look to share with those who will commiserate with us. If we do that, we will continue the path of Israel in Malachi.

Read verses 16–17. Asaph comes to the understanding that there are things he may not understand. Paraphrase what he says in *verse 16.* _

____

Where does Asaph find a renewed perspective of God's goodness, *v. 17*? ____

How would *verses 16–17* be walked out today? _______________

Share a situation where you were fully consumed with what you may have seen as unfair. How did your view change? _______________
What part did God's Word, or his people reminding you of his Word, refocus you? _______________________________________

V.
Again, we need to hide the reality in our hearts that *there is no condemnation in Christ*. We may find ourselves deep in trials of discipline. God's goal is our sanctification.

Read Romans 8:1–4a. What has God done for us through his Son? Paraphrase your answer:

____

Read Romans 8:4b–8. What is the battle we face? _______________

____

Write out verses 7–8. _______________________________________

____

What is the victory cry of *verse 9* for those, *"if indeed the Spirit of God dwells in you?"* _______________________________________

____

"Therefore, sisters, we are debtors, not to the flesh, to live according to the flesh" (v. 12). That is freedom. All we have read in Psalm 73, Malachi, Habakkuk, and experience in life does not need to keep us captive. We are not prisoners to our senses or experiences. If I were teaching this in person, I'd be listening for an *amen!*

Let God minister the truths of this passage in Romans to your heart. Spend time meditating and let your mind be filled with these words of freedom. Remember what Asaph understood. Trying to wrestle with life's complications is just too much to take on. Praise God for his goodness and the reality that he's got you, and he knows what you see and how it challenges you.

Keep persevering!

LESSON SIX

Refocused Perspective

I.

This is our last week. We have studied some important topics. *Psalm 73* catapulted us on a whirlwind of emotions. We should see how easily our focus can be skewed, simply by allowing our senses to concentrate too long on circumstances. Happy news! We also studied how to be refocused, maybe not as easily. Losing our focus on God can come simply by looking too longingly at the world. It takes intention and action to regain a biblical perspective.

We will complete Psalm 73 this week. We will see Asaph come back to a refocused perspective.

Read verses 1–14. This is what Asaph saw. Asaph had an elevated opinion of himself. Let's put that in view *(13, 21–22).* Paraphrase what it says._______________________________________

____

____

Read Romans 12:3 and paraphrase. ________________________________
____

When our perspective is others compared to ourselves, we may come out a bit more righteous. When we compare ourselves to God's requirements, we realize our desperate need.

If I ask you to name a biblical character who experienced self-pity, most people may name Jonah. Elijah experienced self-pity too. Job, Habakkuk, Judas Iscariot are also Bible characters that come to mind when I think of self-pity. *Self-pity* is a deceitful, dangerous, and heart-hardening experience. It cannot be allowed to make a home in our hearts. We see self-pity in Asaph. Thank God, Psalm 73 outlines the steps to freedom.

Hebrews 3:12–14 offers us encouragement and an admonishment. What do you learn? ____
____

God never leaves us to make it up as we go along. He gives us clear directions in his Word. Take the rest of this day to write a prayer of gratitude for all God is teaching you through Asaph. ________________
____

II.

Psalm 73:16–17, paraphrase these verses. ____________________________
____

Psalm 73:18–20, paraphrase these verses. ____________________________
____

Psalm 73:21–22, paraphrase these verses. ____________________________
____

Asaph practiced what Scripture commands. He went into the presence of God and let that refocus him. He wrestled yet came to the end of himself. How can we do that? _______________________________

____

Read *Psalm 27*, which can be found at the end of this lesson. Paraphrase how David comes to the same conclusions as Asaph. ___

____

Let's look at some passages that remind us of God's good supply and how he directs us to keep focused.
*Philippians 4:6–7*_______________________________________

____

*2 Corinthians 5:21*______________________________________

____

*Psalm 100:4–5*____

____

*Colossians 2:6–7*____

____

*Colossians 4:2*____

____

What is learned from these verses? If put into practice, how can these protect you from self-pity?_____________________________

____

____

III.

What I am about to say may cause you to close this study. I do have biblical backing for what I will allege. Here it is: *God wants us to realize the advantages of afflictions.*

Read *Psalm 73:23–28*. Write out Asaph's conclusion. How does this help you? ____

____

Write out *verse 26.* ____

____

To see our afflictions or circumstances as an advantage is not taught from many pulpits. It is not that we should be gluttons for punishment. We are not asked to see ourselves as martyrs. We are just reminded that our afflictions bring about a weight of glory when we walk through them with the right perspective.

What comes from our afflictions?

*Romans 8:18*____

What came from David's afflictions?

*Psalm119:71*____

Afflictions help us remember our duty on earth. What is our duty?

*Micah 6:8*____

____

*Ecclesiastes 12:13*____

____

Exclusively focusing on our duty, we can know, no matter what we are dealing with, God is making us, those who are called according to his purpose in the image of his Son *(Romans 8:28–29). That's a promise!*

IV.

Regaining an understanding of God's goodness is the goal. When we know without a shadow of turning that God is good, we are not easily moved. *Reread Psalm 73. Take time to meditate on verses 27–28. This truth is declared through Scripture. Paraphrase what these passages teach.*

*2 Timothy 2:19*____

____

*Psalm 1:5–6*____

____

*Matthew 25:31–46*____

____

Afflictions, suffering, taking our eyes off God, and seeing the success of those in the world can cause our *"flesh and heart to fail."* At first, *good* was somehow inseparably intertwined with material prosperity, physical well-being, etc. It was worship that taught Asaph that the ultimate good in life is knowing God.

What do you equate "good" with? _______________________________

____

How do you keep from stumbling if you lose what you equate with good? ____

____

V.

You may be thinking, whatever happened to Habakkuk? Well, we do need to look at the final perspective of Habakkuk. Read *Habakkuk*

1:1–4. This is a reminder of where we left Habakkuk. Read a commentary or two to get a background on Habakkuk.

In a sentence, Habakkuk cannot believe God will let the evil nation of Babylon be his tool of discipline on the nation of Israel. His questions were accusatory initially. He gained understanding, though God did not answer his questions directly. God offered this conciliation. What was the conciliation? *Write out Habakkuk 2:4.* ________

____

Read Habakkuk 3:17–18. What is Habakkuk's conclusion? ________

____

Where does this perspective come from? *Verse 19* _______________

____

Remember, if we believe the lie that only good things come to those who love Jesus, we have been taught wrong. We are set up for a devastating stumble. Remember, Eve may have believed that God would not withhold such a pleasant and attractive thing from her. Satan tried to convince God that Job only served him because he was only receiving good things from God.

Read Matthew 4:1–4. What are lessons we can learn from Jesus about dealing with temptations? ________________________________

____

Jesus needed to eat, so why not use his power to get food? Isn't food good?

*Deuteronomy 8:3*______________________________________

____

Even in need of our daily bread, our dependency should be where? *Matthew 6:11*______________________________________

____

Filling ourselves with the knowledge of God before temptations helps us fight them when they come. Ladies, temptations come like a flood. We don't need to fall into them.

Remember, Asaph started with the right view of God. *God is good!* Asaph "almost stumbled" for a moment. He took his eyes off all he knew. He was able to get refocused because of what he reminded himself about God. He didn't seek the answers to his clamoring imaginations. He put himself back in God's presence. He kept his accusations between him and God. He wanted nothing to do with causing others to stumble. He rushed to remember God's perspective of those who are evil from those who are righteous. He was back on track, declaring *God is good!*

Before we finish this study, I want you to write out your testimony. Think about a circumstance where temptation almost caused you to stumble. You quieted the cacophony of complaints rolling through the machinations of your mind with God's Word. You kept your accusations between you and God via a journal or through prayers. You decided not to share your temptation to complain. In the end, you captured your thoughts and refocused on the goodness of God.

____

____

Maybe none of that is true, and you are learning through this study. If that is true, you are still doing well. *Now you know.* It would be best if you began putting these things into practice. Write a prayer asking God to help you *"walk according to your faithfulness"* because there will be a next time to put all this into practice.

____

Thank you for walking through this amazing Psalm with me. I hope you were able to learn and be challenged. Journal things you have learned. How will you choose to let it change you? ______________

____

Now be a doer of the Word as God commands. Don't let this become knowledge that "puffs up!"

That's how you know you persevered!
Blessings! Thanks for taking this trip with me.

PSALM 27
(ENGLISH STANDARD VERSION)

The Lord Is My Light and My Salvation

The Lord is my light and my salvation; whom shall I fear? The Lord is the stronghold of my life; of whom shall I be afraid? When evildoers assail me to eat up my flesh, my adversaries and foes, it is they who stumble and fall. Though an army encamp against me, my heart shall not fear; though war arise against me, yet I will be confident. One thing have I asked of the Lord, that will I seek after: that I may dwell in the house of the Lord all the days of my life, to gaze upon the beauty of the Lord and to inquire in his temple. For he will hide me in his shelter in the day of trouble; he will conceal me under the cover of his tent; he will lift me high upon a rock. And now my head shall be lifted up above my enemies all around me, and I will offer in his tent sacrifices with shouts of joy; I will sing and make melody to the Lord. Hear, O Lord, when I cry aloud; be gracious to me and answer me! You have said, "Seek my face." My heart says to you, "Your face, Lord, do I seek." Hide not your face from me. Turn not your servant away in anger, O you who have been my help. Cast me not off; forsake me not, O God of my salvation! For my father and my mother have forsaken me, but the Lord will take me in.

Teach me your way, O Lord, and lead me on a level path because of my enemies· Give me not up to the will of my adversaries; for false witnesses have risen against me, and they breathe out violence. I believe that I shall look upon the goodness of the Lord in the land of the living!

Wait for the Lord; be strong, and let your heart take courage; wait for the Lord!

CLOSING NOTE

Dear coheirs with Christ,

This study came from a place of struggle for me. That struggle is real and comes up frequently. I wanted an outcome in my life from God, and he chose for it not to be my reality. When I see others with it, I questioned God's goodness.

At one time in my life, I even accused God of being unfair. I thought, *I gave you what you asked for, and this is what I get for that?* There was no sin on my part that kept God from not blessing me with what I wanted. It was simply life and the will of others involved.

I truly felt connected with Paul when he asked God to remove his thorn. God told him no. His grace was sufficient in Paul's weakness. I had to learn that God's grace in the thing I desperately wanted is sufficient for my deepest desire. Over the years, I've learned to desire God more than the thing I wanted so horribly bad.

Now when I see others with this area of life that I thought God owed me, I no longer "almost stumble" or "slip." Instead, I realize, like Asaph, *"God is the strength of my heart and my portion forever."* Living by faith and not by sight has caused me to understand the very gifts in my life are God's good blessings that work his purposes for his glory and my good.

While I know I have not because I ask not, I am careful to ask God to give me the desires of my heart. Literally, to put the desires in my heart that accomplishes his good outcomes. I keep the reality that God is good before my eyes, no matter what life puts in view. *I know I serve a good God.* And what I have is good enough for me. What I don't have, I know he has his reasons.

My prayer for you is that you can come to the conclusions that I have come to. Asaph is our example. God put Psalm 73 in the Bible for our hope. After this study, I pray that you are full of hope.

Blessings in Christ,
Yolanda "Cookie" Doyle

ABOUT THE AUTHOR

Yolanda "Cookie" Doyle has been married for thirty-four years to her husband, Marlon. They call Brookshire, Texas, home. They have five grown children and seven grandchildren. Before moving to Texas in 2018, they lived thirty years in Spanaway, Washington.

God developed her gifts and love for writing and teaching in Washington State. She was in ministry for over twenty years. She began a ministry called Renewed Women, where women received mentoring to help them develop a biblical worldview. She has been a speaker at various women's retreats. Her passion is to help Christians grow up in their salvation. She continues leading Bible studies, biblical counseling, and writing devotions.